The Theology of Karl Rahner

Gerald A. McCool, S.J.

3324

AGI BOOKS, INC.

33 Buckingham Dr.   Albany, N.Y. 12208

This continuing series of booklets makes available to a wide public the best and most articulate thought concerning the problems and perplexities of the present day. Each author is expert in his field and a brief biographical note will be found at the end of this essay.
SBN 87343-027-1

A complete list of the titles in this series is available from the publisher upon request. © Copyright MCMLXI by *Theological Studies* and by Magi Books, Inc. MCMLXIX. All rights reserved.

Printed in the United States of America by the Hamilton Printing Company.

The Theology of Karl Rahner

GERALD A. McCOOL

During the last ten years in a rapidly increasing tempo, the major portion of Karl Rahner's philosophical and theological publications have been made available to American readers. The translation of the seven volume collection of his theological writings, *Schriften zur Theologie*,[1] is now practically complete, and this year the two major philosophical works, *Geist in Welt*[2] and *Hörer des Wortes*,[3] in which, many years ago, Rahner laid down the metaphysical foundations of his speculative theology, have appeared in English form.

Philosophical and Theological Background

One of the strongest impressions left with the reader after his perusal of these books is sheer admiration at the unity and metaphysical coherence of Rahner's thought. Rahner was trained as a philosopher. Under Heidegger at Freiburg he not only made the acquaintance of contemporary existential thought, but, like other German Jesuits who shared this experience, he also discovered the possibility of incorporating much of what is best in contemporary phenomenology and existentialism into a metaphysics of the knowing and willing human subject inspired by Maréchal's *Le point de départ de la métaphysique*. The first fruit of Rahner's experience at Freiburg was his treatise on the metaphysics of human knowledge, *Geist in Welt*. This was followed by his philosophy of religion, *Hörer des Wortes*.[4] After their publication, Rahner, who had been appointed to the chair of dogmatic theology at the University of Innsbruck, turned his attention to theological subjects. The influence of his early philosophical reflection, however, has profoundly influenced his subsequent theological activity. Transcendental anthropology, the discovery of the a priori metaphysical conditions of possibility for the knowing and willing activity of man, the incarnate spirit, had formed the central core of the philosophical speculation concerning the metaphysical structure of man and its relation to a possible divine revelation in *Geist in Welt* and *Hörer des Wortes*. Transcendental anthropology and the metaphysical conclusions drawn from its reflection on the intellectual and volitional activity of the incarnate human person also constitute one of the most obvious threads of unity running through the disparate series of occasional essays which make up the volumes of the *Schriften zur Theologie*. The point of departure and method of reflection characteristic of contemporary Maréchalianism dominate Rahner's theological reflections on the gratuity of the supernatural, the dogmatic concept of concupiscence, the knowability of universal propositions expressing the demands of the natural law, and the need and possibility of a formal existential ethics and moral theology. It is from fundamental metaphysical and theological reflections such as these, whose constant theme is the relation of the free, self-possessing human subject to God and to the world in the cognitive and volitional activity which leads to his self-fulfilment, that Rahner works out to the ecclesiological considerations dealing with the relation between the free, individual person and the hierarchical society of the Church which have drawn so much attention in recent years. Further fruits of these reflections, particularly through the elucidation of the previously neglected categories of personal being, have enabled Rahner to propose more satisfying, though tentative, solutions to a number of thorny problems connected with Christology.

Although there is obviously much more to the theology of Rahner than the endeavor of a Catholic theologian to come to terms with the modern world on the basis of Maréchalian Thomism, one cannot deny that the Maréchalian *Weltanschauung* to which he gave expression in his earlier philosophical works has formed a unifying theoretical element in his theological synthesis. The subjects chosen for discussion, the methods of solution proposed, and the paths charted for future theological development have in large measure been determined by it. This is clearly understood by Rahner's German and Austrian disciples, whose monographs have endeavored to work out in more detail the philosophical and theological synthesis outlined by him. It would seem, therefore, that as interest in Rahner is definitely on the rise in the United States, there is room in an American publication for an outline of Rahner's Maréchalian metaphysics of the human person and its relation to his theological speculation. Armed with this knowledge of the philosophical framework on which Rahner's theological constructions are built, his readers could then approach his individual essays better equipped to appreciate their full significance.

Maréchalian Metaphysics of the Human Person

In *Geist in Welt* Rahner accepts as the starting point for his reflection on the possibility of metaphysics the starting point proposed by Heidegger: the consciousness of man as he raises the most fundamental of all questions, that of the significance of being. As a Maréchalian Thomist, however, it is his aim in reflecting upon this fundamental question to lay bare the a priori conditions of possibility for its appearance in human consciousness. The absolutely unconditioned Pure Act of being, after all, is not one of the material objects of the spatiotemporal world made present to the human subject through the data of sensation; and experience supports St. Thomas' insistence on the fact that man has no direct and proper objective knowledge of entities other than those found in the material, sensible world with which the philosophy of nature concerns itself. Indeed, man is capable of the implicit self-reflection in which he knows himself as a spiritual subject only through the act of affirmation in which he predicates a universal quiddity of a material object given to him in sensible intuition. If, then, the human subject is essentially a "spirit in the world" (*Geist in Welt*), if the human subject is essentially a knower whose conscious possession of himself cannot be achieved in isolation from the act of affirmation through which he distinguishes himself as subject from the material objects of his judgment, how can he become aware of that unconditioned Absolute whose significance is at stake in the most fundamental of all questions, which is, as Heidegger has so well said, the conscious act in which man's authentic structure reveals itself? Since this infinite Absolute cannot enter human consciousness as the content of objective knowledge given in sensible intuition or in the concept, it can only be present to man "unobjectively," as a reality which, although it cannot be represented in objective, conceptual knowledge, is nonetheless grasped by the intellect as the real term of its a priori drive to self-perfection through intentional assimilation of realities other than itself.

Objective judgments would be impossible if the infinite Absolute of being were not present to consciousness in this unobjective manner. For it is its reference to this absolutely unconditioned "horizon" which confers upon the "is" of every judgment the metaphysical necessity which places its affirmation under the laws of being; and it is against the same "horizon," the infinite term of the a priori drive of the agent intellect, that the form of the sensible singular seen in the phantasm appears to the intellect as limited, and hence capable of indefinite repetition in other sensible singulars. For its unobjective grasp of the infinite Pure Act of being enables the intellect to see by contrast the limited character of the sensible form which grounds the capacity of the specific form to repeat itself indefinitely in other individuals; and thus the intellect is enabled to grasp the universal form in the sensible singular presented by the phantasm through a single operation which is at once its abstraction of the universal species and its conversion to the phantasm.[5]

If, then, through its objective judgments the human spirit is implicitly aware of itself as a being which is both intelligent and intelligible, it grasps in the same act the real Infinite which is the fulness of being, and therefore the fulness of intelligence and intelligibility as well. Metaphysics is seen then to be both possible and necessary, even for an intellect whose proper concepts are confined to the essences of sensible objects, because in every judgment the intellect transcends the world of space and

7

time to touch at the term of its a priori drive the infinite unity, truth, and goodness of the unconditioned Absolute, in whose reality every finite object of its affirmation must participate. God, then, as the infinite, intelligent, and consequently free, creative source of all finite reality, is the transcendental condition of possibility for the self-fulfilment of the human spirit through its knowledge of the world.

From this it follows that between God and the human spirit personal relations are possible. Man's will is free because, as an appetite specified by his intellect, it is in its turn a drive toward the infinite Absolute; and so none of the finite participants of God's reality which are the objective terms of its desire can satiate it. God then appears once more as the "horizon," the transcendental condition of possibility, of the free acts in which the human spirit, precisely as free person, tends to self-fulfilment. A free act of the will, however, is more than just a tendency toward an object. An act of the will is free because, unlike the act of an appetite which is wholly determined by the structure of a nature, it is always a self-determination of the spiritual agent, a free stand taken up by him before the objects of his act of acceptance or rejection. What is most precious and important in a free act is not what the agent brings into being in the external world by means of it. Rather it is the attitude which the agent imprints on his own spirit in its fulfilment. For, at its core, each free act consists in an opening or closing of the agent's spirit to an object in the whole context of its presentation, a spiritual attitude of acceptance or rejection whose ground and source cannot be found in the determinism of his nature but only in the positive capacity to say "yes" or "no" to being which is rooted in the dynamic *esse* of a spiritual form intrinsically independent of matter. In the dynamism of every free act, therefore, the human agent, as self-determining person, takes up an attitude to the world of objects which forms the field of exercise for his free decision. More than that, he takes up an attitude toward the absolute Person, the free, creative source of all reality, whose existence as the real term of the a priori dynamism of his will is the transcendental ground of possibility for every free choice. The free, spiritual agent is, according to his essential structure, a finite person taking a stand before the infinite absolute Person.

Philosophy of Religion

Furthermore, if the Absolute of being, truth, and goodness is personal, the innermost depths of that supreme reality can be known by others only in the measure in which He chooses to reveal them in some form of free communication, and in the measure in which a knowing subject can receive and understand the revelation communicated to it by this personal God. Thus, the results of Rahner's transcendental reflection on the conditions of possibility for human knowledge and volition make it evident that the relations between the human person and the absolute divine Person are of such a nature that a free revelation of God's inner personal depths to man is possible, should God decide to give it. Nor is there any reason to place limits on the possible content of such a revelation, since an intellect which is an a priori drive to the infinite Absolute excludes no possible object from the analogous knowledge which it can have of the infinite term of its spiritual a priori by employing concepts whose content of representation has been derived from the objects of man's sense experience.

Man's metaphysical structure, therefore, Rahner tells us in *Hörer des Wortes,* makes him essentially the recipient of a possible divine revelation whose content must be determined by the divine will. Consequently, the function of a philosophy of religion can never be the a priori determination of the content of revelation; it can only be to determine the conditions of possibility for the communication to man of a revelation whose objective content can be known only a posteriori, since it depends on a free decree of God. Its task, therefore, will be to bring these conditions of possibility to light by a closer study of the metaphysical structure of the human subject to whom any possible revelation must be communicated. *Hörer des Wortes,* accordingly, is a continuation of the transcendental reflection on the a priori conditions of possibility for man's conscious activity begun in *Geist in Welt.* In his first book Rahner had already shown that the knowledge of the subject which becomes aware of itself only through affirming a quidditative predicate of a sensible singular is possible only if both the affirming subject and the object of its affirmation are beings whose hylomorphic essence is composed with the accidents of quantity and quality. To become aware of oneself as a subject affirming a sensible object is to become aware of oneself as a being which has become intentionally another being, and one could have become intentionally another being only through becoming the patient in which its transient activity is received. In a reflection which we have not space to follow here, Rahner discovers that such transient activity demands in both agent and patient a hylomorphic essence modified by the accidents of quantity and quality. This enables him in *Hörer des Wortes* to uncover two further essential structures of the human subject. Man is essentially social and essentially historical.

As a form received in matter, the human spirit is by its nature the limited essential act of one of the many individuals who constitute the human species, and who must communicate with each other through the material symbols of speech and cultural artifacts; for these are the signs which carry the personal revelation of their authors through the spatiotemporal world of sensible experience to the intellects of other incarnate persons. The necessity of society, language, and culture has as its ground, therefore, the essential structure which determines the nature of an incarnate person's self-perfection through conscious activity. Furthermore, again as a form received in matter, the self-determining, free human subject must work out his self-perfection through acts of knowledge and free decision which, because of their extrinsic dependence on matter, share the successive character of events in the spatiotemporal world; while, at the same time, the intrinsic independence of matter enjoyed by the self-determining spirit gives to his choices their character of personal uniqueness and unpredictability. Man is not only a temporal and social being; he is essentially historical.

If, then, God should determine to communicate His personal revelation to man, He would be compelled to do so by means of some sensible symbol, a "word," a spatiotemporal perceptible event, which will carry God's message to man. If there is to be a revelation, it must be a unique, historical event. Thus philosophy brings man to the threshold of theology. For if man, by his essential structure, is potentially a "hearer of the word" of God, it is his duty to study his history attentively to see whether in fact God has spoken such a word.

Importance of Transcendental Anthropology

Even in a rapid and perforce superficial sketch of Rahner's metaphysics of knowledge and volition, such as the one given in the preceding paragraphs, the methodological importance of transcendental anthropology in his whole system is very evident. The immutable metaphysical characteristics of man, material reality, and God cannot be determined by a facile process of abstraction, which can do little more than schematize the general characteristics of empirical data. It is very dangerous simply to assume, as too many Scholastics are inclined to do, that such a process of abstraction can be taken without more ado as a valid source of evidence concerning the necessary connection between empirically observed characteristics and the necessary and immutable essences of the sensible singulars of which they are affirmed. Immutable metaphysical characteristics are revealed by a transcendental reflection with discloses their existence as a priori conditions without which experience itself would be metaphysically impossible. The absolute universality of such characteristics has its ground in their unconditioned necessity for the conscious activity of the human spirit as such. There can be no doubt, then, that the structure of man and of the world disclosed in the reflections of transcendental anthropology is the structure of the necessary and changeless essences of things themselves. This epistemological principle, as we shall see, has a decisive influence on the method of inquiry pursued in Rahner's theological studies.

Of great importance, too, for the conduct of Rahner's theological investigations has been the analysis of human experience derived from the transcendental anthropology of *Geist in Welt* and *Hörer des Wortes*. Human experience contains far more than the objective judgment in which the human knower affirms a quidditative predicate of a material sensible object; it contains man's unobjective knowledge of his own personal reality and of the personal reality of the infinite creative source of being. Universal ideas make up an important element of the experience of the reflecting human subject. Sometimes they are mere schematizations of empirical data, but, if they are the result of a transcendental reflection on experience, they can manifest the necessary structure of finite and infinite reality. In the experience of an incarnate person, however, there are also found realities whose fulness eludes expression in the concept and the universal statement. None of the abstract formulations found in universal judgments exhausts the concrete reality of the sensible singular presented to the intellect by the phantasm and in which it sees the universal form. Furthermore, since man is a free spirit whose reality cannot be absorbed into the impersonal determinism of matter, the human subject is capable of experiencing a free encounter with God and finite persons, the fulness of whose concrete content cannot be captured in abstract, general formulas. One of the most important elements in the constitution of man's total experience of reality is, as we have already seen, the unique free attitude which he adopts toward the universe and its creative source in the dynamism of every free decision concerning the objects of the spatiotemporal world. In his considerations on the supernatural, on the natural law, on existential ethics, and on the role of the free individual in the hierarchical society of the Church, Rahner systematically exploits these different levels of human experience, whose full significance could not come to light in a theology dependent on an objectivistic Thomism whose epistemology and metaphysics were derived from a study of inanimate nature rather than from a prolonged reflection on the consciousness of the human subject.

Intellectual Dynamism and the Supernatural Existential

Rahner's philosophy of religion culminated, as we have seen, in his conception of the human spirit as a dynamic reality which can be called, by virtue of its essential structure, an obediential potency for the reception of a divine revealing word. It depends on God, however, whether the word is spoken or whether man is given no further knowledge of the personal Absolute beyond what is contained implicity in the exigencies of the human intellect and will. The whole development of *Hörer des Wortes* is ordered to the delineation of the metaphysical structure which makes the human spirit an obediential potency for revelation; it is never suggested that man, in virtue of his created nature alone, has an exigence or right to receive a manifestation of God's innermost personal life. There is no reason to be surprised, therefore, that even before the unequivocal statements on the subject by Pius XII in *Humani generis,* Rahner took issue with the theologians of the Maréchalian or Augustinian schools who interpreted the a priori dynamism of the human spirit as a natural desire for the beatific vision.[6] In doing so, however, he saw no necessity to abandon the Maréchalian metaphysics of the human person which had formed the core of his philosophical reflections. He did, however, see the need to broaden his philosophical anthropology into a theological anthropology whose speculations would take into account the data of revelation.

Transcendental reflection can distinguish between the merely contingent, empirical characteristics perceived by man in his experience of his own person and the essential structure of his human nature which is the a priori condition of possibility for that experience itself. It is true that a yearning for an immediate encounter with the fulness of infinite personal being has been so interwoven with the experience of man's drive to self-fulfilment in all ages and in all places that philosophers and theologians have identified this longing for a personal vision of God with the essential dynamism of created human nature. Since man is open to a revealing word from God, it would be well, however, to look and see whether revelation has anything to say about the subject. Revelation does have a word to say: it tells us that the beatific vision belongs to that supernatural order which is the effect of a special elevation of human nature to an end essentially beyond its created powers and exigencies. The word of God, accordingly, enables us to acquire an accurate awareness of the limitations of our human nature which man could not obtain by the workings of unaided human reason. The distinction between the essential dynamism of pure human nature and a desire for the beatific vision is a task for theological, not purely philosophical, anthropology.

In the construction of his theological explanation of man's elevation to the supernatural order, Rahner has drawn on the resources of Maréchalian and Heideggerian philosophy. As a true Maréchalian, convinced of the reality of intentional being, he is certain that God's decree elevating man to a supernatural order would be a chimera and not a real decree, if it did not have as its effect the production of a corresponding ontological reality in the human spirit. No purely extrinsic theory of man's elevation, which would leave man's nature metaphysically unaltered by God's positive decree ordering him to a supernatural end, will explain the supernatural satisfactorily. Because of God's decree calling man to a supernatural end, therefore, even before the reception of the first elevating grace, a supernatural reality has been produced in the human soul. Due to that new reality, man's whole spiritual dynamism is now ordered with all its energy to the beatific vision. What name is to be given to this supernatural entity? It is not elevating grace, since it is possessed by every soul, even those of the damned in hell, for it is the metaphysical ground of their searing pain of loss. As an essential structure determining the meaning-giving end of man's most authentic personal activity, it deserves the name Heidegger reserves for the fundamental structures of human consciousness: an existential. Due to God's positive decree, every human soul, before the reception of sanctifying grace, is elevated to the supernatural order by the reception of a supernatural existential, an entity for which it has no exigency, but for which, as spirit, it is an obediential potency.

His theory of the supernatural existential enables Rahner to preserve a great deal of Blondel's fruitful insight that a study of the exigencies of human action must ultimately confront the philosopher with the possibility of an encounter with the God of revelation without compromising the gratuity of the supernatural order as other

Maréchalian theologians had seemed to do. In the dynamism of historical human nature, even though it be deprived of grace, there is always a longing for God which has its metaphysical ground in the supernatural existential. Experience presents the philosopher with a drive which is supernatural; only a theological anthropology, with its more accurate awareness of the limits of human nature, can recognize that drive *as* supernatural.

Theological Anthropology and the Natural Law

Rahner is thus able to draw a distinction between a philosophical concept of human nature and a metaphysical one. In a philosophical concept those essential characteristics of man would be represented which human reason can discover without employing the resources of revelation. The metaphysical concept would contain only those characteristics which are essential elements of human nature. Both the contingent and the supernatural would be rigorously excluded. In the light of Rahner's theory of the supernatural existential, it is clear that, in his opinion, a theological anthropology alone can furnish such a metaphysical concept of human nature. The exact determination of the content of this metaphysical concept of human nature, moreover, is a task of no small moment for the Christian moralist and for the Christian theologian, for it is the metaphysical essence of man which is the ground of the rights and obligations of the natural law.[7] Unhappily, the facile generalization of experience indulged in all too frequently by our Christian moralists can never result in the abstraction of a truly metaphysical concept of human nature. In experience there is much that is contingent and much that is conditioned by the historical state in which man finds himself. Because a characteristic has been associated with man up to the present, it does not follow that this characteristic is part of his changeless essence. The Christian moralist has the lesson of history to teach him that. It is part of the task of the Christian philosopher and theologian, therefore, to continue the transcendental reflections on the necessary a priori conditions of human experience as such which were initiated in *Geist in Welt* and *Hörer des Wortes*.[8] It is not enough to know that man is necessarily and changelessly a being who is spiritual, social, and historical. Much more must be learned about his metaphysical essence, if we are to ground the demands of natural-law morality. As a sign of what he hopes may be accomplished, Rahner himself attempts to establish by such a transcendental reflection of human experience that it belongs to the metaphysical essence of man to be a member of a species whose origin must be found in a single wedded pair.[9] Yet he is not entirely convinced that the method of transcendental reflection by itself will be able to constitute a metaphysical concept of human nature whose comprehension is wide enough to ground in man's absolutely changeless essence all the propositions of natural-law morality. Some way must be found, he believes, of joining empirical observation to the transcendental reflection on the conditions of possibility of human experience. It must be one of the chief preoccupations of Scholastic philosophers to discover whether in this way the results of empirical observation can share to some degree in the necessity which up to the present has been the exclusive property of propositions derived by the method of transcendental reflection.[10]

Theology of Concupiscence

The metaphysics of human knowledge which he worked out in *Geist in Welt* and the metaphysics of human freedom developed in *Hörer des Wortes* made it possible for Rahner to provide an original and very satisfying answer to another problem connected with the relations between nature and grace: the content of the dogmatic concept of concupiscence.[11] The Platonic type of thinking which would identify concupiscence with the sensible appetite whose drive to the things of earth resists the pull of a spiritual appetite which is by its nature a drive toward the things of heaven cannot be squared with the metaphysics of human knowledge and desire. The human spirit is not only a subsistent act; it is also the form of a body-soul composite. From the soul, as the radical specifying principle of being and activity, emanate both the sensible and intellectual faculties through which the total man comes into contact with his world. In the experience of the body-soul composite, therefore, there can be no such thing as purely sensible knowledge in which the intellect plays no part at all; in a knower who cannot think without conversion to the phantasm, and whose intellect has as its proper object the essences of material beings, there can be no such thing as purely spiritual knowledge. If man's knowledge is never purely spiritual, it follows that his tendency toward the goods he knows can never be a purely spiritual desire. Sensible objects, therefore, are known and desired in a sensory-spiritual fashion; and spiritual objects are known and desired in a spiritual-sensory way.

Nor can one square with the metaphysics of the will the theory which would identify concupiscence with the spontaneous desires of the will which in man's present state necessarily precede the act of free election. Each free act of the will, as we have already seen, has as its essential core the act of self-determination by which the agent takes up a position toward a finite exterior object presented to him for his acceptance or rejection. In the finite agent, the taking up of such an attitude necessarily involves a transition from potency to act. Such a transition, however, in order to be possible, presupposes that the faculty through which such an attitude is taken up was not always in possession of the object. The object, therefore, must have been presented to the will itself, and not just to the intellect; otherwise the will, which is an essentially different faculty, could not have made the transition from potency to act in relation to it. In a faculty, however, which is by its nature an active tendency toward an object (not just a faculty of passive receptivity like the intellect), the presentation of an object can only take place through a spontaneous movement of the faculty toward it. From this analysis it follows that the indeliberate acts which precede the act of free election belong to the necessary nature of the human will. They are an indispenable condition of possibility for any deliberate act of that faculty. Consequently, the essence of concupiscence cannot consist in the presence of these spontaneous motions of the will without which even Adam before his fall would have been incapable of eliciting a free act.

The metaphysics of human freedom developed in *Hörer des Wortes* does more, however, than simply bring to light the inadequacy of these erroneous theories concerning the comprehension of the dogmatic concept of concupiscence. It enables the theologian to determine accurately what the positive content of that concept must be. In the dynamism of every free act, as we have already seen, the agent takes up a free attitude toward the absolute Person, since no human good can be accepted or rejected except in virtue of the dynamism of the will toward this infinite fulness of goodness. Furthermore, from the analysis of the human person carried out in *Geist in Welt* and *Hörer des Wortes* it is clear that the fundamental characteristic activity of the human person is self-possession through spiritual activity. Through his intellect the person possesses himself by means of the perfect reflection which in the judgment enables the subject to distinguish himself from the object of his affirmation. Through his will the subject possesses himself in the autodetermination of his own self contained in the free disposition of his person, the adoption of an attitude, in relation to the finite objects of the world and to God, the ultimate "horizon" made present to him through the dynamism of every choice. But just as there are many elements of the body-soul composite which cannot be captured in the person's self-possession by means of his intellect, so too a large part of man's affective dynamism, his sense desires and the spontaneous motions of his will which have their roots in his nature and in his acquired virtues and vices, refuse to be taken into the personal disposition of the agent, the free attitude adopted by him toward an object in a single act of free decision. This resistance of man's spontaneous affectivity (which Rahner in this context calls his "nature") to his "person" in his endeavor to dispose of himself completely in the engagement to an object or a person effected through his free decision is the reality designated by the term "dogmatic concupiscence." Dogmatic concupiscence is not necessarily an evil thing. It prevents a human being from making the total, irrevocable commitment of his whole being to evil of which the pure angelic spirit is capable; and it is the source of the instinctive resistance to an evil choice offered by the spontaneous movements of the will which check a virtuous man on his course toward sin and summon him to repentance after he has fallen. In Adam, then, the gift of integrity consisted, not in the absence of the spontaneous movements of his affectivity, but rather in the lack of any resistance on their part to his total disposition of himself in an act of free decision. Its purpose was not to make sin less difficult; for it actually carried with it the peril of a graver and more fully deliberate offense to God than the sin of which a man is capable when the force of his choice is weakened by the movements of concupiscence. Rather, its aim was to make Adam more fully that free, self-possessing source of action which is the human person, and to include the driving energy of his whole being in the unimpeded commitment for or against the absolute Person involved in his free choice of good or evil. If integrity, therefore, was the reason for the gravity of Adam's sin, the concupiscence which followed it was the ground of possibility for his repentance. Its spontaneous resistance to his choice against his Creator deprived his will of that fixity in evil which is the mark of the fallen spirit. Offering an opening for the grace of contrition, the motions of concupiscence explain why Adam's fallen nature was an obediential potency for redemption.

Situation Ethics

Rahner's metaphysics of the human subject has not only enabled him to deal successfully with the dogmatic problems of grace and nature; it has enabled him to engage in fruitful dialogue with the proponents of contemporary situation ethics.[12] Existential philosophy and contemporary Protestant theology have joined forces to create an extreme form of situation ethics. No general rules, no universal laws of conduct, whether their claim to validity be based on the essential structure of human nature or on the data of revelation, are admitted by its adherents as obligatory norms for the free decisions of the individual human subject. In his most authentic depths, where his true freedom resides, each human subject is confronted with his incommunicable uniqueness. He finds himself alone before the call of God in the experience of his unique situation. General norms may be a useful guide for his understanding of it, but he cannot hope to take refuge in them from his personal responsibility to answer in sincerity and faith the individual call given to him by God in the exigencies of this unrepeatable situation. Transcendental anthropology makes it evident, however, that man is not just an irreplaceable individual. He is a member of the human species, whose essential structure can be known, to some degree at least, through a philosophical reflection on the a priori conditions of possibility for man's spiritual activity, and through the revealing word of God which, as Rahner's philosophy of religion has made quite clear, can be given to man, not only in the incommunicable depths of his individual heart, but in an exterior historical event whose essential significance is accessible, in principle at least, to every member of the human species. General laws, drawn from reason and from revelation, can and do exist; and there is neither philosophical nor theological justification for a theory of morality which refuses out of hand to accept the validity of the line of reasoning through which a man can know with certainty that his situation, for all its uniqueness, is one of the "cases" covered by a universal moral law.

There is much to be said for situation ethics, however, for all of its extremism, because it is a timely reminder to the Christian moralist that up to the present he has been content all too often with an ethics and a moral theology of general laws alone. Although it reveals the falsity of their exaggerations, the essential structure of man's nature supports the claim of the existentialist theologians that there are situations in which the subject is confronted with an obligatory expression of the will of God whose ground is not a universal law but the demands of his unique and utterly personal situation. As a subsistent, immortal form, capable of a personal encounter with the infinite God, the human subject is more than merely a limited iteration of a specific form in a material composite. The Greek theory of the unimportance of the individual can never do justice either to the being or to the activity of the free, self-possessing source who reaches his full perfection through an encounter with the absolute Thou in the dynamism of a responsible free decision about the individuals presented to him in unique situations. God is the God of individuals. There is no reason therefore, to believe that the attitude to be taken up toward God in every personal choice should be determined exclusively by the general specific structure of the agent's action and be in no way affected by the unique context of an individual situation. Nor is there any reason to imagine that any one of several courses of action which must be called permissible as far as the general laws of morality are concerned is *eo ipso* equally conformable to the will of God manifested in this concrete situation, and that the choice of any one of them at all will express the attitude toward God and toward the world which this situation should bring into being in the agent as a result of his free decision. There is need, then, for the Catholic philosopher and the Catholic theologian to complement their reflections on the natural law by the development of a formal existential ethics; for, although obviously there can be no science of the individual moral choice in its unique singularity, one can penetrate more deeply into its nature in a manner analogous to the general formal metaphysics of the individual which is found in Scholastic ontology. Some of the topics which should be made the objects of investigation in such a formal existential ethics would be: the manner in which the moral conscience is aware of the individual action; the interpenetration of knowledge and volition in the operation which gives rise to our understanding of another person; and the nature of man's fundamental option in the stand toward the world which reveals itself as already taken up when he begins a conscious reflection on his moral life. Interesting as these considerations are for their own sake, they are even more interesting because of the direct connection which Rahner makes between them and his speculations on the nature of sin and on the role of the free individual in the Church.

In the general run of theological manuals sin is dealt with as an offense against a universal law laid down by God. Would not the development of a formal existential ethics enable the theologian, without neglecting that aspect of sin, to go beyond it?[13] Sin's character as a betrayal of God's personal love and as an offense against a personal imperative grounded in the individual's unicity could then receive more adequate treatment in our dogmatic theology. And would not such a formal existential ethics also furnish our dogmatic theology of the supernatural with the categories which it requires to do justice to the personal encounter with the personal God in the supernatural love which is charity?

The Free Person in the Church

Ecclesiology would also benefit from a greater exploitation of the metaphysics of the human person.[14] From his theological anthropology, Rahner has established that man, according to his unalterable metaphysical structure, is a free, incarnate spirit who must work out his destiny by sharing in the historical process of a spatio-temporal world. As a member of a species of incarnate persons, he is essentially social and can reach his self-fulfilment only through cultural contact with other persons in the societies of the family and the state. Elevated to the supernatural order by the supernatural existential, he is called to personal union with God in charity, and through God's revealing word he knows that he can reach his supernatural end only through union with Christ in His Mystical Body, the external, social, historical reality which is the hierarchical Church.

Yet, although the Church is a true society with a fixed structure of genuine hierarchical authority which touches its members "from without," her rulers may never forget that a society is made up of persons, whose dignity consists in their inviolable freedom.[15] In a society whose aim it is to bring its members to perfection, authority can never be unmindful of the fact that the perfection of a human act lies not in what is accomplished exteriorly but in the free attitude adopted by the agent who accomplishes it in the fulness of his personal liberty. Compulsion should not be substituted lightly for the opportunity of personal choice.[16] Furthermore, in a society whose *raison d'être* is to bring its members to a personal encounter with God in charity, and in which the members are capable of perceiving a personal divine obligation whose ground is found, not in a general norm binding all the members of the society as such, but in the depths of their personal unicity, the workings of the charismatic spirit can never be absent.[17] The authorities of the Church would be doing violence to the nature of man and to the supernatural order if they were to endeavor to confine the inspiration of the Holy Spirit to the general pronouncements of an ecclesiastical bureaucracy.[18] The very nature of man and of the Church demands that room be left for individual inspiration on the part of the individual layman within the society of the Church, or on the part of the individual religious within the society of his institute. After all, the Church is not called holy merely because she is the custodian of universal norms of sanctity; she is holy, too, because she has always been the mother of the individually different saints.[19] From all this it follows that in the local and parochial apostolate "orders from the top" should not crush out those free groupings of individuals within the Church who are following the inspiration of the Holy Spirit in works that have not been formally organized and technically incorporated into the legal structure of the parish or the diocese.[20] And although the individuals within the Church would do violence to the nature of the society of which they are members if they were to disregard the legitimate directions of hierarchical authority, the wielders of that authority in turn should be attentive to the workings of the Holy Spirit in the individual consciences of the faithful and seek to profit from them by providing an adequate means of expression for a sane and ordered public opinion in the Church.[21]

Development of Dogma

The influence of Rahner's metaphysics of the human person on his ecclesiology is not confined to the theology of the apostolate. The philosophy of human knowledge worked out in *Geist in Welt* provides an avenue of approach to the question of the development of dogma.[22] Man, as spirit in the world, always possesses a total personal experience, composed of objective and unobjective knowledge, a concrete awareness and interpretation of his total world of persons and of things which is too rich to permit its rapid and easy explication in a series of conceptual judgments, expressing through clear, sharply-defined universal concepts the different aspects of reality which the intellect has seen in the concrete individual. It is through the psychology of progressive conceptualization of a knower's total experience rather than through the logic of implicit deduction, which is operative only on the conceptual level, that the theologian should endeavor to explain the historical evolution of the Church's teaching. On the basis of this psychology, he will be able to explain how the rich total experience of the concrete Christ possessed by the apostles has gradually been explicated in the consciousness of the Church in a growing body of conceptual formulizations evolved in the course of her existence under the influence of the Holy Spirit.

Philosophy of the Person and Christology

The preoccupation of modern phliosophers with the human subject as the free personal source of conscious action has raised a problem concerning the mediatorship of Christ whose solution cannot be found by a simple repetition of the traditional formula "one person in two natures." [23] For the modern philosophy of the person calls into question the very possibility of the assumption by the Logos of a human nature such that it would enable Christ to perform the functions of a veritable human mediator. To fulfil that office, Christ, as an authentic man, aware both of His humanity's union with the Logos and of His creaturely status, must elicit from the depths of His human liberty the acts of adoration and obedience which express the perfect attitude of the free human subject toward God and toward the world. How is it possible for the human spiritual center of Christ to possess that perfect autonomy through which Christ, as the most perfect human being, stands freely vis-à-vis the Logos as a human mediator before His God, and still belong to the Logos as an element of the hypostatic union? If Christ, by reason of His human nature, has such an autonomous disposition of His whole being through an attitude of authentic liberty, then to the modern philosopher the human nature of Christ is a person and so cannot be assumed by the Person of the Logos.[24] To this modern difficulty a modern answer must be found; and Rahner finds it by applying to Christology the theology of God's creative action. God alone, as the creative cause of being, has the capacity to constitute by His creative, dynamic presence the very autonomy of a being other than Himself. The metaphysics of the human spirit has also shown most clearly that the higher a reality is placed in the scale of perfection through its spiritual self-possession, the more profound and intimate is the presence in it of the divine Being. In fact, the human spirit is through its essential dynamism an obediential potency for an even more intimate presence of the Divinity than that which its natural powers would make possible. Following such a line of reasoning, we can see how suitable it is that a divine Person who has created the most perfect human autonomy (which is by its very nature an obediential potency to transcend itself and touch the infinite in the immediate vision which is its supernatural end) should give to this creature in which is found the highest perfection of human liberty the divine presence which corresponds to it by assuming that perfect liberty to His own person in the hypostatic union.[25]

The awareness of Christ's human consciousness of the union of His human nature to the Logos, Rahner believes, need not be explained in terms of any special grace communicating to His human intellect an objective knowledge of the Logos to whom it is united. From the metaphysics of knowledge worked out in *Geist in Welt* we know that a spiritual reality is both intelligent and intelligible. A reality such as the union of Christ's spirit to the Logos is therefore intelligible and could not fail to enter into the unobjective knowledge which Christ possessed of His own human spirit as self-possessing source of conscious action. This unobjective awareness of its union to the Logos is given to Christ's human intellect as an immediate ontological consequence of the hypostatic union.[26]

Theology of the Sacred Heart

The solution of these two problems in Christology has encouraged Rahner to believe that great progress can be achieved in that branch of theology by a systematic exploitation of the theology of creation and of the resources placed at the theologian's disposal by the existential reflection on human consciousness which is a prominent feature of modern philosophy.[27] If the hypostatic union is the summit of creation, as we have seen, would it not be possible to gain a greater understanding of Christ by examining more carefully His relation to the total movement of creation in which, under the Old Alliance, His coming was prepared, and whose process He has made part of Himself through the Incarnation which has made Him the plenitude and end of temporal history? In Rahner's outline of a theology of the Sacred Heart we have some indication of the use which he would make of the metaphysics of the person in the development of Christology.[28] Drawing on the resources of his reflections on human consciousness, Rahner sees the devotion to the Sacred Heart as an expression of divine worship which touches the Person of our Lord in the deepest center of His total being, in the union of His body, soul, and divinity. It is this deepest center of our Lord's total being which gives its form to the basic attitude with which He faces the fallen world, an attitude of love, human and divine, freely given with His grace to sinners. This attitude which shines forth from the life and sufferings of the concrete Christ experienced by the Christian in his contemplation of the history of salvation provokes in his personal depths in turn the free attitude of agnition, the loving response to the concrete reality of Christ's Person which men call devotion.

An Experiential Thomism

The outline of Rahner's theology sketched out in the preceding pages—even though it is far from complete[29]—makes it evident that his work is the product of an original and unified thought. His approach to theology has been determined by the nature of the philosophical instrument which he fashioned for himself in *Geist in Welt* and *Hörer des Wortes*. That philosophy is authentically Thomistic, but, unlike the Thomism of a previous generation of philosophers and theologians, the focus of its reflections is primarily, almost exclusively, the interior life of the human subject. In the tradition of the existentialist phenomenology which he learned to appreciate through his contact with Heidegger at Freiburg, Rahner's philosophy draws upon the results of a careful discrimination of the various levels of human knowledge and affectivity together with their corresponding objects; and in the tradition of Maréchal, his philosophy employs as its primary method a transcendental reflection on the conditions of possibility for man's spiritual activity. His system is, in other words, a philosophical anthropology.

Philosophical Difficulties Against Rahner's System

The affinity of his philosophical reflections to the preoccupations and methodology of contemporary German philosophy, and the remarkable fruitfulness of their results in the development of a theology which is at once traditional and compatible with the thought processes of contemporary non-Catholic religious speculation, have secured for Rahner a position of great prestige and influence among German Scholastics. In both their philosophical and their theological monographs, and in their manuals as well, the influence of his teaching and writing can often be discerned. More time, however, will have to elapse before the permanent results of his philosophical and theological system can be definitively determined.

In both his exploitation of the various levels of human experience and his application of transcendental anthropology to the solution of philosophical and theological problems, Rahner has achieved immediate success and has pointed the way to further happy results which can be anticipated from a wider application of his method. Time alone can tell whether or not these happy results will actually come to pass. Although the discrimination of the various levels of experience has already borne good fruit in Rahner's theology of the individual in the Church, the great result anticipated from that source, the constitution of the urgently-needed formal existential ethics, remains a promise rather than a *fait accompli.* And whether or not it is in the power of transcendental anthropology to furnish sufficient information about man's changeless essential structure to enable the ethician to ground on its results the universal judgments of our natural-law morality remains an open question. Except for the attempted a priori grounding of monogenism through transcendental anthropology and a brief sketch of a similar justification of the credibility of Christ's revelation by the same method,[30] neither Rahner nor his disciples have gone very far beyond the basic structures of human nature outlined in *Geist in Welt* and *Hörer des Wortes.* Nor has Rahner done anything to carry further his vague suggestion that transcendental deduction might be broadened in its scope by uniting it to some process of empirical abstraction.

A serious objection, however, which many American Thomists will present to the theology of Rahner is its great dependence on the a priori Thomism of Maréchal. For many of their number Maréchal's philosophy is an object of extreme distrust. Neither the discovery of the absolute Infinite as the term of the a priori dynamism of the human spirit nor the deduction of man's hylomorphic structure from the exigencies of his knowledge appears to them to have been sufficiently grounded by the proponents of the Maréchalian system. To accept as the starting point of one's philosophical reflection the content of human consciousness as such and to determine the end of philosophical investigation as the discovery of the a priori conditions of possibility for the data of consciousness is simply to initiate once more the critical reflection of Kant; and there is no reason to believe, in the opinion of many modern Thomists, that the logical result of such a critical reflection can be anything else than the adoption of the critical idealism of Kant himself.[31] To this objection Rahner can reply only by inviting his critic to examine carefully the philosophical reflection carried out in *Geist in Welt*. If the metaphysical conclusions reached in that book are justified by the philosophical method employed in it, then its author has won the right to proceed with his theological anthropology; but if, on the other hand, they are not so justified, then, despite its individual successes in dealing with one problem or another, his theological anthropology as a systematic theological method will be doomed to failure.

Rahner's theological system, however, whatever be the ultimate judgment passed upon his anthropology, will remain as one of the great metaphysical theologies of our century. Its originality and boldness, its completely different character from earlier Thomistic syntheses, such as, for example, the synthesis of Cardinal Billot, is another proof of the remarkable vitality of Thomistic metaphysics, and of the capacity which Thomism possesses to enter into dialogue with modern thought while remaining faithful to its original genius. It is to be hoped that an opportune translation of Rahner's other major works will give to a larger number of American theologians, within and without the Church, the opportunity to come to grips with his rich and original metaphysical theology.

Notes

¹ *Schriften zur Theologie* (7 vols.; Einsiedeln, 1954–1966). English translation, *Theological Investigations* (London-Baltimore, 1961–   ). The first volume of the English translation contains an excellent introduction by Cornelius Ernst, O.P. locating the transcendental Thomism of Rahner in the movement of modern thought from Kant to Heidegger. A brief but excellent introduction to Rahner's theology can be found in the paperback by Herbert Vorgrimmler, *Karl Rahner, His Life, Thought and Works* (Glen Rock, N.J., 1966). A longer but eminently readable introduction can be found in Donald Gelpi, S.J., *Life and Light: A Guide to the Theology of Karl Rahner* (New York, 1966).

² *Geist in Welt* (Munich, 1957). English translation, *Spirit in the World* (New York, 1968). The first edition of *Geist in Welt* was published in Innsbruck in 1939.

³ *Hörer des Wortes* (Munich, 1963). English translation, *Hearers of the Word* (New York, 1968).

⁴ An earlier edition of *Hörer des Wortes* was published in Munich in 1941.

⁵ The theory of abstraction through a single operation of the intellect which is at once the abstraction of the species and the conversion to the phantasm is one of Rahner's contributions to the metaphysics of knowledge. Not only is it the central theme of *Geist in Welt* but it has been employed by theologians influenced by Rahner in their speculative theology. See the author's "The Primacy of Intuition," *Thought* 37 (1962) 57–73.

⁶ "Über das Verhältnis von Natur und Gnade," *Schriften zur Theologie* 1, 323–45; *Theological Investigations* 1, 297–317. For a discussion of Rahner's theology of the supernatural order, see J.P. Kenny, S.J. "Reflections on Human Nature and the Supernatural," *Theological Studies* 14 (1953) 280–87. See also L. Malevez, S.J., "La gratuité du surnaturel," *Nouvelle revue théologique* 75 (1953) 561–86, 673–89.

⁷ "Bemerkung über das Naturgesetz und seine Erkennbarkeit," *Orientierung* 19 (1955) 239–43.

⁸ *Ibid.*

⁹ "Theologisches zum Monogenismus," *Schriften zur Theologie* 1, 253–322, esp. 311–22; *Theological Investigations* 1, 229–96, esp. 286–96. Since then, this position has been re-thought and substantially modified in "Evolution and Original Sin," *Concilium* (June, 1967).

¹⁰ "Bemerkung über das Naturgesetz und seine Erkennbarkeit," pp. 242–43.

¹¹ "Zum theologischen Begriff der Konkupiszenz," *Schriften zur Theologie* 1, 377–413; *Theological Investigations* 1, 347–82. For an excellent discussion of Rahner's theology of concupiscence, see J.P. Kenny, S.J., "The Problem of Concupiscence: A Recent Theory of Professor Karl Rahner," *Australasian Catholic Record* 29 (1952) 290–304; 30 (1953) 23–32.

¹² "Über die Frage einer formalen Existentialethik," *Schriften zur Theologie* 2, 227–46. This is a noteworthy article, not only because of Rahner's remarks on existential ethics, but also because of the connection which he makes between the metaphysics of the human person and his reflection on the role of the free individual within the Church.

¹³ *Ibid.*

¹⁴ *Ibid.*

¹⁵ "Würde und Freiheit des Menschen," *Schriften zur Theologie* 2, 247–77; *Theological Investigations* 2, 235–263.

¹⁶ "Die Freiheit in der Kirche," *Schriften zur Theologie* 2, 95–114; *Theological Investigations* 2, 89–107. Furthermore, the personal decision in favor of the Absolute Person, springing from the fundamental attitude of man as incarnate spirit toward the world and its horizon, the Absolute Person, can lead to an implicit but truly supernatural faith on the part of many "anonymous Christians" who explicitly disclaim any association with the visible, hierarchical Church. For an excellent treatment of Rahner's theology of the "anonymous Christian," see A. Röper, *The Anonymous Christian* (New York, 1966).

¹⁷ "Über das Laienapostolat," *Schriften zur Theologie* 2, 339–73; *Theological Investigations* 2, 319–352. Rahner develops this theme at greater length in a subsequent article, "Das Charismatische in der Kirche," *Stimmen der Zeit* 160 (1957) 161–86. It is also the

topic of the chapter, "The Charismatic Element in the Church," in *The Dynamic Element in the Church* (New York, 1964). For a further development of the role of the individual in the Church, see *Nature and Grace* (New York, 1964), pp. 9–38.

[18] "Würde und Freheit des Menschen," *Schriften zur Theologie*, 2, p. 274; *Theological Investigations* 2, p. 260. The theme of the unique call of Christ to the free commitment of the individual Christian runs through Rahner's development of the spiritual exercises of Saint Ignatius. See *Spiritual Exercises* (New York, 1965). For an illuminating interpretation of the Ignatian "discernment of spirits" through the use of Rahner's metaphysics of human knowledge, see *The Dynamic Element in the Church*, pp. 84–170.

[19] "Die Kirche der Heiligen," *Schriften zur Theologie* 3, 111–26; *Theological Investigations* 3, 91–104.

[20] "Friedliche Erwägungen über das Pfarrprinzip," *Schriften zur Theologie* 2, 299–337; *Theological Investigations* 2, 283–318. For a further developmen of this theme, see *The Christian Commitment* (New York, 1963), pp. 75–113.

[21] Öffentliche Meinung in der Kirche," *Orientierung* 15 (1951) 255–58. Public opinion in the Church is also the theme of Rahner's book, *Free Speech in the Church* (New York, 1959).

[22] "Zur Frage der Dogmenentwicklung," *Schriften zur Theologie* 1, 49–90, esp. 81–90; *Theological Investigations* 1, 39–77, esp. 68–77.

[23] "Probleme der Christologie von heute," *Schriften zur Theologie* 1, 169–222; *Theological Investigations* 1, 149–200.

[24] *Ibid.*: *Schriften* 1, esp. 178–82; *Theol. Invest.* 1, esp. 157–61.

[25] *Ibid.*: *Schriften* 1, esp. 182–86; *Theol. Invest.* 1, esp. 162–65; 176–85.

[26] *Ibid.*: *Schriften* 1, esp. 189–92; *Theol. Invest.* 1, esp. 168–71.

[27] *Ibid.*: *Schriften* 1, esp. 187, 192–93; 206–22; *Theol. Invest.* 1, esp. 166, 171–72, 185–200.

[28] "'Siehe dieses Herz': Prolegomena zu einer Theologie der Herz-Jesu-Verehrung." and the following article, "Einige Thesen zur Theologie der Herz-Jesu-Verehrung," *Schriften zur Theologie* 3, 379–415; *Theological Investigations* 3, 321–352.

[29] Nothing has been said, for example, about Rahner's theology of death which is adumbrated in "Probleme der Christologie von heute" and given fuller treatment in a subsequent article, "Zur Theologie des Todes," *Zeitschrift für Katholische Theologie* 79

(1957) 1–44, and in the book *On the Theology of Death* (New York, 1961). An English translation of the *ZKTH* article can be found in *Modern Catholic Thinkers,* ed. A. Robert Caponegri (New York, 1960). For a further development of Rahner's theology of death, see Ladislaus Boros, S.J., *The Mystery of Death* (New York, 1965).

Another important element of Rahner's theology, closely connected with his Christology and his anthropology, is his theology of the priesthood. Rahner has dealt specifically with the priesthood in the third volume of his *Theological Investigations,* in his *Spiritual Exercises* and in numerous articles. One of the most moving presentations of Rahner's vision of the priesthood is found in the article, "The Faith of the Priest Today" *Woodstock Letters* 93 (1964) 3–10. For Rahner's views on the formation of future priests, see "Über die theoretische Ausbildung künftiger Priester heute, *Stimmen der Zeit* 175 (1964–65) 173–93 and "The Student of Theology: The Problems of His Training Today," in *Theology for Renewal: Bishops, Priests, Laity* (New York, 1964), pp. 119–46.

Rahner's theological productivity has been prodigious. A list of his writings on the philosophy of religion and on dogmatic, pastoral and ascetical theology which was drawn up in 1954 contained 299 titles. Rahner's activity has not diminished in the intervening years.

[30] "Probleme der Christologie von heute," *Schriften 1,* pp. 206–9; *Theol. Invest.* 1, pp. 185–189.

[31] For a clear and forceful summary of the difficulties connected with the Maréchalian starting point and method in philosophy, see E. Gilson, *Réalisme thomiste et critique de la connaissance* (Paris, 1939) pp. 130–55. In recent years a number of Amercan philosophers have expressed their uneasiness concerning the validity of transcendental reflection as a method of grounding metaphysics through the thematization of the *a priori* structure of the dynamism of the human spirit. The transcendental method, according to these philosophers, is not as rigorous, critical and free from presuppositions as the philosophers in the Maréchalian tradition assume. In the determination of metaphysical categories much more attention must be paid to the work of English and American linguistic analysis and to the work of Heidegger and of Merleau-Ponty. For an incisive presentation of these difficulties, see M. Novak, "Lonergan's Starting Place: The Performance of Asking Questions," in *A*

Time to Build (New York, 1967) and the articles of R. Hinners, E. MacKinnon, S.J. and B. Nachbar in *Continuum* 6 (1968) 221–224, 225–231, 232–235. For a clear explanation and defense of transcendental Thomism, see E. Coreth, *Metaphysics* (New York, 1968) and O. Muck, *The Transcendental Method* (New York, 1968).

Related works published by Magi Books, Inc. *Studies in the Psychology of the Mystics*, Joseph Maréchal, 350 pages, $3.75. *The Philosophy of Karl Rahner*, Joseph Donceel, $.50. *Contemporary Philosophy of Religion*, J. P. Mackey, $1.00.

The Author

Gerald A. McCool, S.J., is Associate Professor of Philosophy at Fordham University. He holds Licentiates, both in philosophy and theology, from the noted Woodstock College and his Doctorate from Fordham University.

His studies in the realms of the philosophy of religion, the thought of Henri Duméry, and Transcendental Thomism are well known and have appeared in such journals as: *Thought, International Philosophical Quarterly, Theological Studies, Continuum,* and *The Modern Schoolman.*

At present he is engaged on a work in the important but neglected field of those philosophers in the tradition of Maurice Blondel, and the application of Christian dialectical philosophy to theology and spirituality.

The editors of this series are grateful to Professor McCool and to *Theological Studies,* in which this essay first appeared, for permission to make it available to a wide public.